ELT Development Series

SERIES EDITOR Thomas S. C. Farrell

T0155336

Teaching Vocabulary

Michael Lessard-Clouston

tesolpress

www.tesol.org/bookstore

TESOL International Association
1925 Ballenger Avenue
Alexandria, Virginia, 22314 USA
www.tesol.org

Group Director, Content & Learning: Myrna Jacobs
Copy Editor: Meg Moss
Cover Design: Citrine Sky Design
Design and Layout: Capitol Communications, Inc.

ISBN 9781945351945
eBook ISBN 9781945351952
Library of Congress Control Number 2019956809

Table of Contents

Series Editor's Preface

The *English Language Teacher Development (ELTD)* series consists of a set of short resource books for ESL/EFL teachers that are written in a jargon-free and accessible manner for all types of teachers of English (native, nonnative, experienced, and novice). The ELTD series is designed to offer teachers a theory-to-practice approach to second language teaching, and each book presents a wide variety of practical approaches to and methods of teaching the topic at hand. Each book also offers reflections to help teachers interact with the materials presented. The books can be used in preservice settings or in in-service courses and by individuals looking for ways to refresh their practice. Now, after nearly 10 years in print, the ELTD series presents newly updated, revised editions that are even more dynamic than their first editions. Each of these revised books has an expanded number of chapters, as well as updated references from which various activities have been drawn and lesson plans for teachers to consider.

Michael Lessard-Clouston's revised edition of *Teaching Vocabulary* again explores different approaches to how teachers can teach vocabulary in second language classrooms. Michael has added two new chapters on "Technology and Online Resources for Vocabulary Learning and Teaching" and "Using Word Lists in Vocabulary Teaching: Options and Possibilities." He has also updated the references and research, new web links, and added more Reflective Questions as well as new activities throughout the book, as well as lesson plans teachers at various levels can consider. This revised edition is again a valuable addition to the literature in our profession.

I am very grateful to the authors of the ELTD series for sharing their knowledge and expertise with other TESOL professionals to make these short books affordable for all language teachers throughout the world. It is truly an honor for me to work again with each of these authors for the advancement of TESOL.

Thomas S. C. Farrell

Acknowledgments

This revised and expanded edition has benefited from the input of many people. I am indebted to Birgit Harley for her wonderful OISE/UT seminar on vocabulary learning and teaching, which led to my passion for and research in this area. At Biola University, I have taught a graduate vocabulary learning and teaching course for over a decade, and I am grateful to my students who used the first edition of this book and thus helped expand my understanding of the joys and challenges of teaching and learning English and its vocabulary. My sons, Joel and Caleb, always provide encouragement and new insights on vocabulary that I appreciate, and Tom Farrell, series editor extraordinaire, offered comments and suggestions I valued that pushed me to produce a much better book. Final thanks to TESOL Press for its professionalism and attention to detail!

CHAPTER 1

Vocabulary and Its Importance in Language Learning and Teaching

This book is about vocabulary teaching, but it is first necessary to establish what *vocabulary* means to focus on teaching it. This introductory chapter reminds you of the importance of vocabulary in language learning and teaching.

What Is Vocabulary?

Throughout this short book, I hope to engage you directly in thinking about English vocabulary and the teaching of it to students learning English as a second or foreign language. As you begin, please stop and answer the question asked in the header above.

REFLECTIVE QUESTION

● My definition(s) of English vocabulary:

Your answer likely has something to do with the *words of a language*, which is perhaps how most people think of vocabulary, and that is correct because vocabulary does deal with words. Yet, vocabulary is much more than just single words, as this book will demonstrate. Recent vocabulary studies draw on an understanding of *lexis*, Greek for "word," which in short means all the words in a language. So it will probably not surprise you to learn that vocabulary here also includes *lexical chunks*, phrases of two or more words, such as *Good morning* and *Nice to meet you*, which research suggests children and adults learn as single lexical units. Phrases like these involve more than one word but have a clear, formulaic usage and make up a significant portion of spoken or written English language usage. Also called *formulaic sequences* (Alali & Schmitt, 2012) or *multiword expressions*, they are thus central to English vocabulary learning and therefore worth teachers' attention as they teach vocabulary (Webb & Nation, 2017).

REFLECTIVE QUESTIONS

- What are some lexical chunks or multiword expressions you feel your students should know? How might you teach them in a class?

So, vocabulary can be defined as *the words of a language, including single items and phrases or chunks of several words that convey a particular meaning, the way individual words do.* Vocabulary addresses single lexical items—words with specific meaning(s)—but it also includes lexical phrases and multiword expressions.

The Importance of Vocabulary

Vocabulary is central to English language teaching because without sufficient vocabulary, students cannot understand others or express their own ideas. Wilkins (1972) writes that "while without grammar very little can be conveyed, without vocabulary *nothing* can be conveyed" (pp. 111–112). This point reflects my experience with different languages; even without grammar, with some useful words and expressions, I can often manage to communicate. Lewis (1993) goes further to argue, "Lexis is the core or heart of language" (p. 89). Particularly as students develop greater fluency and expression in English, it is significant for them to acquire more productive vocabulary knowledge and to develop their own personal vocabulary-learning strategies.

Students often instinctively recognize the importance of vocabulary to their language learning. As Schmitt (2010) notes, "learners carry around dictionaries and not grammar books" (p. 4). Teaching vocabulary helps students understand and communicate with others in English. Voltaire purportedly said, "Language is very difficult to put into words." I believe English language students would concur, yet learning vocabulary also helps students master English for their purposes.

REFLECTIVE QUESTION

- What are some specific ways that you observe that vocabulary is important to your students?

Aspects of Vocabulary Knowledge

The concept of a *word* can be defined in various ways, but teachers need to be aware of and focus on three significant aspects: *form*, *meaning*, and *use*. According to Nation (2020), the *form* of a word involves its pronunciation (spoken form), spelling (written form), and any word parts that make up this particular item (such as prefix, root, and suffix). An example of word parts can been seen in *uncommunicative*, where the prefix *un-* means *negative* or *opposite*; *communicate* is the root word; and *-ive* is a suffix denoting that someone or something is able to do something. Here, they all go together to refer to someone or something that is not able to communicate, hence *uncommunicative*.

Nation (2020) states that *meaning* encompasses the way the form and meaning work together; in other words, the concept and what items it refers to, and the associations that come to mind when one thinks about a specific word or expression. *Use*, Nation (2020) notes, involves the grammatical functions of the word or phrase, collocations that normally go with it, and, finally, any constraints on its use, in terms of frequency, level, and so forth. *Form*, *meaning*, and *use*, Nation (2020) declares, have both a receptive and a productive dimension, so knowing these three aspects for each word or phrase actually involves 18 different types of lexical knowledge, as summarized in Table 1.1. When teachers teach vocabulary to build students' knowledge of words and phrases, helping them learn any and all of these different components assists them in enhancing their English vocabulary knowledge and use.

Table 1.1 What Is Involved in Knowing a Word

Aspect	Component	Receptive knowledge	Productive knowledge
Form	Spoken	What does the word sound like?	How is the word pronounced?
	Written	What does the word look like?	How is the word written and spelled?
	Word parts	What parts are recognizable in this word?	What word parts are needed to express the meaning?
Meaning	Form and meaning	What meaning does this word form signal?	What word form can be used to express this meaning?
	Concepts and referents	What is included in the concept?	What items can the concept refer to?
	Associations	What other words does this make us think of?	What other words could be used instead of this one?
Use	Grammatical functions	In what patterns does the word occur?	In what patterns must this word be used?
	Collocations	What words or types of words occur with this one?	What words or types of words must be used with this one?
	Constraints on use (register, frequency . . .)	Where, when, and how often would we expect to meet this word?	Where, when, and how often can this word be used?

Source: Adapted from Nation (2020, p. 16)

After you have looked through Table 1.1, please consider your students' particular strengths and weaknesses with English in terms of these three aspects of vocabulary knowledge.

REFLECTIVE QUESTION

- My impression of my students' strengths and weaknesses with English vocabulary:

    Strengths   *Weaknesses*

Each person's response here will vary, as vocabulary knowledge is very personal. Some teachers are very good at the grammatical functions of particular words or phrases, for example, and others have a strong knowledge of English word parts. I want to encourage you to begin with your students' strengths, because everyone has some vocabulary knowledge relevant to English, even if it derives from his or her own native language. Aim to build on learners' strengths and also recognize various weaknesses. For example, many students read in English and thus may be adept at recognizing meaning in terms of concepts and referents, but if they have not heard the words and phrases they are reading, they may be weak at recognizing them when they hear them spoken or weak at pronouncing them when they read out loud. Sometimes students learning English as a foreign language (EFL) are weaker than English as a second language (ESL) learners at recognizing particular constraints on vocabulary usage, such as the fact that only young people use a particular word or expression, which might be colloquial and not usually deemed appropriate in more formal contexts such as speeches. Yet, if teachers are aware of their students' strengths and weaknesses in English vocabulary, then they have a place to start to expand students' knowledge and strengthen weaker areas.

Perhaps as you reflect on the information in Table 1.1, you find the task of teaching English vocabulary a little daunting. If so, you are not alone! Teachers and students need to learn much to understand and use words and phrases correctly in different situations. This book does not claim to cover it all, but instead aims to help you understand important issues from recent vocabulary research and theory so that you can approach teaching vocabulary in a principled, thoughtful way. It will also help you reflect on vocabulary teaching in your particular context and on how you might improve your vocabulary teaching.

Developing a Love for Vocabulary Learning

As a changing, growing reality, English vocabulary is challenging. As Ur (2012) aptly states, unlike grammar, "lexical items . . . are an open set, constantly being added to (and lost, as archaic words gradually go out of use)" (p. 3). Perhaps this situation is most evident with computer-related vocabulary, like the *internet*, *email*, and *web browser*, which was not commonly used even 20 years ago. Now, though, everyone seems to know these items and how important such realities are to their lives and work. English vocabulary's expansion is exciting, but it also means that teachers and students alike need to be in the habit of learning vocabulary.

People can expand their English vocabulary knowledge in many different ways. As a native English speaker, I have been learning vocabulary for many years, but I am still a learner because English vocabulary changes and grows. Occasionally, I come across an unknown word or phrase (or a new usage for one I already know) in something in print or online, or on the radio or television. I stop to consider what it might mean in that particular context and make a guess. If I have a dictionary close by, I will check it for the word or phrase, or if I am at my computer I will check an online dictionary. Words and phrases fascinate me, and if new ones seem useful, then I may later use them in my own speech or writing—even if it is to comment on this new vocabulary item! Whatever your personality and learning style, both teachers and students can develop a growing love for English vocabulary learning and naturally share a passion for words and phrases in any language.

REFLECTIVE QUESTIONS

- What aspects of English vocabulary currently interest you?

- What two or three strategies for learning English words and phrases do you model and teach?

One resource that teachers can explore to model and teach English words and phrases is the website WFP Freerice at https://beta.freerice.com /categories/english-vocabulary, which calls itself "the world's only vocabulary game that feeds the hungry." It is also available as an app. Through the World Food Programme (WFP), this site allows those with internet access to check their vocabulary knowledge using multiple-choice questions. For every correct answer, 10 grains of rice are donated through the WFP to help feed the hungry. You might bookmark this site and share it with your students.

Teaching Vocabulary

Learning vocabulary is essential to English language use and "a critical part of developing second-language competency" (Barclay & Schmitt, 2019, p. 2). Many excellent books focus on learning English as an additional language, including those by Horst (2019) and Nation (2013). But the English teacher definitely plays a role, so this book addresses vocabulary teaching. As Webb and Nation (2017) discuss, the teacher's role is multifaceted, involving selecting words to be learned, developing a vocabulary learning program, explicitly teaching words and choosing materials that incorporate the target vocabulary, designing activities that allow for vocabulary use and fluency development, as well as helping students become proficient with vocabulary learning strategies and measuring their learning. While this short book cannot address everything, it should help teachers understand important points and reflect on them in relation to their students and their teaching.

Conclusion

English vocabulary is complex, with three main aspects related to form, meaning, and use, as well as layers of meaning connected to the roots of individual words. Teaching vocabulary is not just about words; it involves multiword expressions, knowledge of English vocabulary, and how to go about learning and teaching it, which the next chapter explores.

REFLECTIVE QUESTION

- What is something important you learned about vocabulary from this chapter?

CHAPTER 2

A Second Language Perspective on Understanding Vocabulary

This chapter develops a more detailed second language (L2) perspective in teaching vocabulary to English language learners (ELLs). It addresses the grammar/vocabulary relationship, word families, personal aspects of vocabulary knowledge, and three kinds of English vocabulary.

Grammar and Vocabulary

English language teaching often distinguishes grammar and vocabulary. This distinction can be useful, but as Lewis (1993) declares, teachers should remember that "language consists of grammaticalised lexis, not lexicalised grammar" (p. 51). You may not know much grammar, but if you know some vocabulary you can still communicate. Vocabulary teachers should recognize the *lexicogrammar* of language—the way that grammar and vocabulary work together to enable English language users to communicate effectively. Mirroring how Nation (2020) discusses *form*, *meaning*, and *use*, other applied linguists also use these three aspects of language usage in their discussions of lexicogrammar.

Zimmerman (2009) reminds us that "grammar provides important information about meaning, and meaning determines how a word is used" (p. 55). It is thus helpful to let students know if a word being taught is a noun, a verb, an adjective, or an adverb, for example, and any special information about it, such as whether the noun is countable or if a verb always takes a complement and, if so, what type, such as verb plus infinitive, gerund, or either of these. Unfortunately, most English for speakers of other languages (ESOL) teacher training programs tend to neglect vocabulary, but emphasize grammar. I hope this book will help such programs and guide readers to understand and teach as though grammar and vocabulary are not at odds with one another. Instead, they work together, which teachers must help students understand. Vocabulary may not always be quite as clear-cut, right or wrong, as grammar. Even with good grammar skills, English language learners will not be able to communicate effectively without sufficient English vocabulary knowledge and learning strategies.

REFLECTIVE QUESTIONS

- Take a moment to reflect on a word or phrase that you recently taught, and think about any important grammar and vocabulary connections using these questions:
  - What part of speech (e.g., noun, verb, adjective, adverb) is the word?
  - Does the word have any irregular or unexpected forms?
  - Collocations: Does the word or phrase typically follow particular words, or precede certain others (such as complements)?

Did you address any of the Reflective Questions as you taught the item you thought of? Teachers should be aware of these issues when they teach new vocabulary. As Zimmerman (2009) observes, how difficult it is to learn certain words varies, depending on whether they take irregular plural or past forms, and nouns and verbs appear easier to learn than adjectives and adverbs. As much as possible, teachers can indirectly teach that a noun is countable by using *a* or *an* with it (e.g., *an apple*) and that a word is a verb by introducing it in the infinitive form (e.g., *to organize*). Ideally, teachers should give students example sentences when introducing new vocabulary to provide as much context and as many clues as possible. A teacher might write, for example, *The student offered her teacher an apple before she helped him to organize the desks in the classroom.* Then he or she can read the sentence out loud or have a student do so, so that the class has opportunities to interact with the form, meaning, and use of these two target vocabulary items. Zimmerman (2009) also recommends that teachers train students to understand and use the grammatical information included in their dictionaries and offers some suggestions for doing so, particularly for information that will help students practice using new words.

REFLECTIVE QUESTION

- In what ways do (or could) you help your students make connections between English grammar and vocabulary?

Word Families

From an L2 perspective, with vocabulary it is helpful to think of *word families*, which are sets of related word forms starting with a base or root word (with one main meaning) plus its *inflected* forms and derivations (Nation, 2013). Inflected forms often relate to verb forms, such as *-s*, *-ed*, and *-ing*, but inflections and derivatives usually concern affixation in English, mentioned in discussing prefixes and suffixes with *uncommunicative* in chapter 1. So, for *observe*, the word family includes the inflections *observes*, *observed*, and *observing*, plus the derivatives *observation*, *observable*, *observant*, and *observer*. Some word forms in this word family occur more frequently than others, but they all relate to the root word *observe*. Teachers should indicate, however, that different meanings for the same written form, such as *pupil* (a student or the center of the eye), are considered different words in this view. Most research today assumes that students who know one member of a word family will have some access to the others, but this is not necessarily always the case, so teachers should not make that assumption. English language students are often unaware of these distinctions, so teaching them common prefixes and suffixes in English will help them expand their vocabulary knowledge.

This task will often lead you to your dictionary, and on this one
occasion, a hard-copy dictionary may trump an electronic one. Most
electronic dictionaries may only offer one short entry, whereas in a hard-
copy dictionary, the noun *a friend* or the verb *to friend* will be followed
by *friendless*, *friendly*, and *friendship*. As this example indicates, a printed
dictionary allows you to glimpse one or two pages of entries at a time, but
it nonetheless tends to show word forms in a word family created using
suffixes. It does not normally reveal the related forms created with prefixes,
such as *to befriend* or *to unfriend*.

In my experience, it can be helpful to teach common, related forms
together, such as *a friend* (noun), *to friend/to befriend* (verb), and *friendly*
(adjective). It also helps to ask students about where they have seen these
items used, as in *to friend* or *to unfriend* someone on the social networking
service Facebook. I do not try to teach every member of a word family
at once, but sometimes, advising students whether a related noun, verb,
adjective, or adverb form exists can be helpful. For instance, *friendly* is a
common adjective, *friendly* is not commonly used as an adverb anymore,
and in sports, the noun *a friendly* means a game played for practice rather
than to win. Students can also write this kind of information on vocabulary
cards or in their vocabulary notebook, which are two other key vocabulary
learning strategies.

Vocabulary Knowledge Is Personal

Two important distinctions for vocabulary knowledge are worth reviewing.
First, some vocabulary is expressive, or *productive*, and used in speaking
or writing, and some is *receptive*, which is used to understand or associate

meanings in reading or listening. Table 1.1 in chapter 1 reflects this distinction, with questions concerning receptive and productive vocabulary knowledge and use.

The second distinction is *breadth* (i.e., quantity, the number of words known) versus *depth* (i.e., quality) of knowledge of a word or phrase, its form, meaning, use, and so forth. Because vocabulary knowledge is personal, individuals possess various degrees of knowledge of specific lexical items. Typically, however, learners have greater receptive vocabulary knowledge and more breadth than depth knowledge of individual words or phrases. Students tend to develop more productive vocabulary knowledge based on their receptive knowledge of words or phrases. Similarly, they usually increase their depth of vocabulary knowledge of individual items as they use words and phrases in writing and speaking, as well as through reading or listening.

REFLECTIVE QUESTIONS

- Answer these questions about your students' vocabulary knowledge.
  - What types of vocabulary do your students need productive knowledge of? What kinds of words can they get away with simple receptive knowledge of?
  - In what aspects of English vocabulary do students need to develop more depth of vocabulary knowledge? How might you help them do so?

Some topics and activities call for specificity and thus require productive knowledge of relevant vocabulary for speaking or writing. Other subjects require simply the understanding of particular items. Your students likely have a wide breadth of vocabulary knowledge but only know a small number of words and formulaic expressions for which they have a great depth of vocabulary knowledge. This is normal but may also encourage you to help students develop greater depth knowledge of words and phrases they already know.

Everyone has specific hobbies or areas of expertise and likely knows some specialist or technical vocabulary. My son, for example, has belts in judo and jiu-jitsu, and, as a result, he has receptive and productive knowledge of various terms for particular throws, holds, and moves in those sports. You can encourage students by helping them recognize some areas of expertise where they can easily learn English terminology and teach it to others. Many young people, for example, are familiar with computer and social networking vocabulary and can quickly learn it or use it in English.

REFLECTIVE QUESTIONS

- In your classes, what types of specialist knowledge do your students typically have? How might they transfer this knowledge into their English vocabulary usage? Consider students' hobbies, sports, and other areas of expertise.

Connecting with students' previous knowledge and experience as they approach lessons in a new language is always useful. Everywhere I have taught, I have discovered that students like to talk about their hobbies and other areas of interest and expertise. Nowadays, the internet allows students to find English language blogs, videos, and texts that relate to their passions, such as cooking, baseball, or traveling. Developing their English lessons and homework so that students can connect knowledge in these areas to their presentations, journaling, and so forth has many benefits. How might you go about working on personal aspects of vocabulary with your students?

Three Kinds of English Vocabulary

The dominant approach to vocabulary in English language teaching is based on frequency of use because the vocabulary of English is so large (Schmitt & Schmitt, 2014). Essentially, this *frequency approach* suggests that teachers should teach students the most common words in English first, so that they will have the most frequently used words at their disposal.

Research over the years has drawn on *corpora*, large collections of texts, to analyze English vocabulary, resulting in three main levels of frequency. According to Schmitt and Schmitt (2014), the field of teaching ESOL typically addresses these three main kinds of vocabulary: high-frequency, mid-frequency, and low-frequency English words. Most *high-frequency* vocabulary is on West's (1953) general service list (GSL) of 2,000 words plus Coxhead's (2000) academic word list (AWL) of 570 items common in academia. Those and newer important lists are discussed in more detail in chapter 6. However, reading for pleasure, watching television, or comprehending most English language textbooks, requires some understanding of *mid-frequency* vocabulary (Schmitt & Schmitt, 2014). This ranges from around the 3,000– to 9,000–word frequency levels, with the higher number being the beginning of *low-frequency* English vocabulary.

Based on this division, vocabulary specialists suggest ensuring that all students learn general, high-frequency words first, as they are the most useful. For English language students preparing to study at college or university in English, common academic vocabulary is highly recommended, as is learning some *technical* vocabulary of their chosen academic discipline. Research on technical vocabulary suggests each field has several hundred technical words and phrases, but that they also fall into the three levels— high-, mid-, and low-frequency English vocabulary, with discipline-specific meanings and uses (Lessard-Clouston, 2010). And, because low-frequency vocabulary represents many thousands of words, Webb and Nation (2017) and others recommend students develop vocabulary-learning strategies to deal with low-frequency words as they come across them in reading and listening.

REFLECTIVE QUESTIONS

- A word's frequency is key to understanding its usefulness and pedagogical relevance.
    - Visit the Frequency Trainer at https://www.lextutor.ca /freq/train/ to take a quiz on the frequency of 10–15 words, rating whether each belongs to the 1,000–2,000, 3,000– 5,000, 6,000–10,000, or 11,000–15,000 frequency bands in English.
    - How is your vocabulary "frequency intuition"?
    - Consider whether your students know, should know, or are likely not to need to learn these words at this stage.

To choose appropriate words and phrases for students to study and learn, teachers must understand the high-, mid-, and low-frequency levels of vocabulary in English. Unfortunately, McCrostie's (2007) research indicates that "teachers cannot always identify the most frequent words in the English language and should consult frequency lists in conjunction with their intuitions" (p. 62). So, if you struggled with some of the words in the Reflective Questions, you are not alone! As McCrostie suggests, it is best to check word frequency lists, rather than simply rely on intuition. While useful books exist, easily accessible frequency lists are available online.

Conclusion

This chapter outlined four topics to introduce a fuller L2 perspective on English vocabulary: the grammar-vocabulary connection, English word families, the personal nature of vocabulary knowledge, and three main kinds of English vocabulary.

REFLECTIVE QUESTIONS

- Please read the following vignette and then answer the questions.

Vignette 1: Vocabulary Teaching

Roberta *is an ESOL teacher at an adult school connected with a community center language program in a metropolitan area in the United States. Although many of her students are from Spanish-speaking contexts, she also has some learners from Asia and Europe, and a few from the Middle East and Africa. Their ages range from about 20 through 50 years of age. She is teaching false beginners (students who have already studied English at some point before) an integrated skills course, using a popular textbook from a major publisher of materials for ESOL in the United States. She enjoys using a communicative approach in her lessons and because her students are all adults, Roberta likes to integrate cultural and social aspects of English language use into her classes.*

— As you reflect on Roberta's situation, what is similar to and different from the classes and students you teach? In what ways do you think teaching vocabulary would be easy or difficult in this context? Why?

— What issues from this chapter do you think could perhaps help inform Roberta's vocabulary teaching?

CHAPTER 3

Research Into Practice: 10 Tips for Vocabulary Teaching

This chapter gives a synopsis of 10 major research findings that offer English language teachers clear tips for putting them into practice in their vocabulary teaching.

Choose Frequent, Relevant Words to Teach

Teachers should choose frequent, relevant words to teach. As noted earlier, currently the dominant view is a frequency perspective on English vocabulary because frequency seems to be the best overall criterion for determining which words to focus on teaching. In essence, "more frequent words tend to have greater value than less frequent words, because they are more likely to be needed for communication" (Webb & Nation, 2017, p. 6), which is why most textbooks emphasize general and academic vocabulary. Although various frequency lists exist (and the most important ones are discussed in chapter 6), the words teachers choose to teach should be relevant to their students, based on their teaching objectives and students' proficiency level. If students are beginners, they need to master the first 1,000 items on a general service list, or perhaps the 800 items on the Essential Word List; the AWL or another specialist list is simply beyond them. With low-intermediate students, emphasizing the 2,500 to 2,800 words from a New General Service List (see chapter 6) is appropriate.

But . . . Not All Vocabulary Is Created Equal

From a learning perspective, not all English vocabulary is created equal, however, because at least three levels of word frequency exist, discussed in chapter 2, and the learning burden of a word or phrase involves how easy or difficult it is for students to learn and use. In summary, for pronunciation and meaning, the learning burden is heavier for longer words, as well as for words for abstract concepts, *polysemous items* (words with multiple definitions), and *false friends* (words similar in form to words in the student's first language [L1], but different in meaning or use).

In addition to teaching frequent, relevant words, teachers need to help students learn to reflect carefully on the words they will invest time in studying. Barker (2007, p. 528) recommends that students look for answers from teachers, native speakers, or dictionaries to three main questions: Is this a common word? Is it useful for someone at my level to learn? Is there a particular reason I should learn this word now? If teachers choose frequent, relevant words to focus on in class and in homework, then they offer a good model for students; however, students need to take responsibility for their learning, too, especially outside of class. They also need to know some words are harder to learn than others, yet those useful or relevant are worth the effort.

REFLECTIVE QUESTIONS

● What vocabulary do you need to help your students acquire? High-, mid-, or low-frequency words? What kinds of words should you teach?

● How do you help your students take responsibility for their vocabulary learning? Might you use Barker's (2007) three questions with them?

Deliberate Vocabulary Teaching Is Key

Over the years, research has revealed that while people can and do learn word meanings incidentally, such learning most often does not come easily and may not be very effective (Webb & Nation, 2017). For ESOL, then, vocabulary teaching is important, and part of a teacher's job is to incorporate deliberate vocabulary teaching into classes to help students develop the breadth and depth of vocabulary knowledge required for them to use it effectively, both receptively and productively. As Webb and Nation (2017) indicate, although deliberate vocabulary teaching mainly contributes to just one of their four strands of a balanced vocabulary learning program, it also assists students in consolidating and expanding on their English vocabulary gains (p. 226). Such a program requires explicit vocabulary teaching: giving attention to particular words and phrases; conveying what is involved in knowing a word or phrase; using various types of vocabulary practice activities and review exercises in class and for homework; using materials that contain the target vocabulary; and giving frequent, repeated attention to vocabulary during every class so that students are able to use and develop fluency with it.

Vocabulary Learning Is Incremental

Deliberate vocabulary teaching is necessary because research clearly shows that vocabulary learning is an incremental process, due to both the sheer number of lexical items students encounter (and the vocabulary size they will need) and the detailed knowledge they need to develop of specific lexical items (Barclay & Schmitt, 2019). Remember the various aspects of vocabulary form, meaning, and use outlined in Table 1.1? Learning all those components does not come all at once, thankfully, but takes place over time. Research indicates that such aspects of word knowledge seem to go from zero to partial to more precise development, and teachers want to help students understand this as they approach their English vocabulary learning. As Barclay and Schmitt (2019) declare, "word learning is a complicated but gradual process" (p. 8). As a result, students should spend some time studying and reviewing their word cards, and words in their vocabulary notebooks or on their vocabulary app each day, rather than cramming for a vocabulary quiz. Students can add to their entries on word cards and in vocabulary notebooks (assuming they leave space) as they learn more about words and phrases they are studying. Such activities reflect and allow for the incremental nature of vocabulary learning. One useful scale moves from receptive to productive word knowledge and is outlined in Table 3.1.

Table 3.1 An Incremental Scale of Knowledge of Words and Phrases

I have never seen this word before.	I have seen the word but am not sure what it means.	I understand the word when I see or hear it in a sentence.	I have tried to use this word, but I am not sure I am using it correctly.	I use the word with confidence in either speaking or writing.	I use the word with confidence in both speaking and writing.

Source: Zimmerman (2009, p. 116)

Teachers can help students understand the incremental nature of vocabulary learning and will ideally help them move along (left to right) this scale of word knowledge as they meet, understand, and start to use new words and phrases, so that they fully master them.

REFLECTIVE QUESTIONS

- What are one or two specific ways that you can deliberately teach vocabulary in one of the classes you offer?

- Think of how your knowledge of a specific word has grown over time (perhaps a multidefinition item). Write out how you can use this example with students in a particular class.

Teach Vocabulary-Learning Strategies

Partly because vocabulary learning is a process, students need active vocabulary-learning strategies that they use for learning and reviewing new words and phrases (Webb & Nation, 2017), both on their own and in class. Yet, teachers should model and practice vocabulary learning strategies in their classes as well as ask students to use them there and elsewhere. In a Test of English as a Foreign Language (TOEFL) preparation course, for example, I introduced and modeled a new strategy that students could use to build their vocabulary knowledge, which is crucial for success on any important test. In other courses, in going through a reading together the students practice using contextual clues as they come across words with which they are unfamiliar, and I have written words on the board and asked students to break them down into prefixes, roots, and suffixes, brainstorming potential meanings. Students in my classes have used dictionaries to examine what they say, not only about a word's meaning, but also regarding its form and usage. These strategies, as well as using word cards, are highly recommended. Yet, in my experience, students will be more likely to use such strategies if they see in class how they will help improve their vocabulary knowledge and use.

Vocabulary Practice Is Necessary to Enable Productive Use

Although many factors influence vocabulary knowledge, practice is necessary for learners to move receptive knowledge into productive use (as in Table 3.1). Schmitt (2010, p. 26) states, "the more a learner engages with a new word, the more likely he/she is to learn it." Receptive knowledge is important, but if students do little more than read or hear a new word, they are unlikely to remember it, let alone use it. If, however, students interact with the word (say or write it) and think about its meaning and any similarities (grammatical, etc.) to other words they know, then the incremental learning discussed here is more likely to happen. For this reason, Schmitt (2010) concludes that "virtually anything that leads to more exposure, attention, manipulation, or time spent on lexical items adds to their learning" (p. 28). How can you help your students to engage more with the English vocabulary they are learning?

REFLECTIVE QUESTIONS

- What vocabulary learning strategies do you model in your classes? How can you teach such strategies more systematically in one course?

- What activities do you use in class to help students practice new vocabulary? What are some additional ways you can encourage students to engage with new words and phrases?

Provide Many Exposures to New Vocabulary in Class

The learning and practice noted here require many exposures to new words and phrases, and this should therefore be a teacher's major goal. Estimates for the number of times a student needs to encounter a new word to learn it vary widely, but 10 to 20 exposures to new words and phrases have been found effective for learning many of the aspects of vocabulary knowledge in Table 1.1 (Schmitt, 2010, p. 348). As Folse (2011) states, "The single most important aspect of any vocabulary practice activity is not so much what ELLs do with the word but rather the number of times ELLs interact with the word" (p. 364). Folse thus recommends that teachers model and encourage many uses and retrievals of words they are teaching through short interactions with students about such words in class. This might include writing the word on the board along with other new vocabulary items, asking students questions about the words, concepts, or different categories (e.g., people, actions, adjectives) for the words in question, and posing personal questions that require students to think about these lexical items. Teachers can also encourage students to write such words down in sentences in their notebooks, listen to and repeat their pronunciation, use them in dialogues in class, and so forth.

Textbooks Seldom Address Vocabulary Sufficiently

Teachers need to ensure students frequently encounter new words and phrases in their courses because textbooks seldom address vocabulary sufficiently. Brown (2011), for example, analyzed nine commonly used ESOL textbooks and the vocabulary activities in them. Of the aspects of vocabulary knowledge in Table 1.1, Brown (2011) found that the most prominent focus was almost uniquely on form and meaning, with vocabulary use receiving much less attention. Thus, word parts, associations, concepts, collocations, and constraints on vocabulary use were seldom addressed. Brown (2011) notes, "For teachers the main implication . . . is that they should take responsibility for ensuring that their learners have opportunities to learn about the different aspects of vocabulary knowledge" (p. 94).

Teachers should also *not* expect students to learn a significant amount of vocabulary from their textbooks. O'Loughlin (2012) studied the vocabulary in three levels of a popular EFL textbook series for vocabulary input and concluded that over the course of 3 years of using these texts, a relatively small percentage of GSL and AWL items would be introduced. He therefore concludes, "It is necessary for the teacher to guide learners to study words which are useful, and provide information on . . . deliberate learning strategies" (O'Loughlin, 2012, pp. 264–265).

REFLECTIVE QUESTIONS

- Consider a particular lesson you teach. What are 5 to 10 vocabulary items it requires you teach? And what are several specific ways you can provide students with different types of exposures to these words?

- Examine your current textbook. What does it say about the vocabulary included? What aspects of Table 1.1 do you see addressed in activities and exercises? Which seem to be neglected?

Deliberate Vocabulary Learning Is Important Too

Students in English language classes must be involved in a deliberate vocabulary-learning program to acquire the amount of English vocabulary required for them to become proficient speakers and writers on topics important for them to communicate about. As Folse (2011) argues, "the most successful learners are those who have a very specific concrete plan of action and consistently carry it out" (p. 365). Part of the teacher's job is to help students develop such a plan. This may involve extensive reading, which typically uses graded readers with a controlled number of vocabulary items in them to enable students to read for pleasure without encountering too many unknown words (see Extensive Reading Central, https://www.er-central.com). Although this typically requires an extensive library of books at varied levels, nowadays such programs might also involve various online resources. One I appreciate is Read Oasis, https://readoasis.com/, which emphasizes learning English through stories and the power of big ideas made accessible to learners. It enables students not only to read short or long texts, but also, in some cases, to listen to such texts or to watch short videos about related topics. The free content on that site is useful, and students who find it helpful can pay to access the whole site.

Any Unfamiliar Word or Phrase Is Worth Explaining

Given all the suggestions in this book, it is worth stating that in English language teaching, any word or phrase that students struggle to understand in class is worth the teacher's attention. As Horst (2019) rightly declares, "In classroom vocabulary teaching, any word that seems unfamiliar to a group of learners is worth explaining" (p. 131). As noted at the start of this chapter, teachers should choose frequent, relevant words to teach in class, recognizing that not all words are created equal, so deliberate vocabulary teaching is key. But students become frustrated when they cannot understand what a listening or reading activity is about because they do not know a key word or phrase. Sometimes a short explanation, gloss, or even an L1 translation will help students quickly understand and be able to focus once again on the task at hand. If these items are found on any of the important, well-designed word lists introduced in chapter 6, they are worth precious class time to explain, if not explicitly incorporate into a lesson plan. If students want to say or write something but need a particular English word or phrase, again it is worth the teacher's attention to quickly take time in class to help them understand the options in a dictionary. Words or phrases that students find essential to comprehension and production need to be explained or provided, even if they are not on a famous word list. The teacher should let students know if a word seems archaic, but helping them understand and use any word useful to them should be a priority.

REFLECTIVE QUESTIONS

- Think of a particular course you teach. What steps can you take to help students develop a deliberate vocabulary learning program? Think of tasks students can use to practice vocabulary related to your course.

- Can you think of an occasion in a lesson where you needed to explain or gloss a challenging word or phrase? How did you handle it? What are some potential ways you might now address unfamiliar words in class?

Conclusion

This chapter has outlined 10 tips for teaching vocabulary based on research findings and offered questions to help readers think about applying them in their teaching. Vocabulary learning is important, and vocabulary teaching can and should support it. Teachers thus need to know their students and their vocabulary needs, which the next chapter explores.

CHAPTER 4

Getting to Know Your Students and Their Vocabulary Needs

To teach students vocabulary effectively, you must know them and their English vocabulary needs. This chapter offers some suggestions and four steps to take. First, please take time to answer the following questions about one class you teach.

REFLECTIVE QUESTIONS

- Think of your students' background, education, and language proficiency. What vocabulary knowledge do they have at this point? What vocabulary knowledge should they have?

- Consider your students' learning goals and your course objectives. Do students need to learn academic vocabulary (for reading, etc.)? To be able to listen to lectures? To write short essays? To pass a specific test?

Step 1: Determine Your Students' Vocabulary Level

The first step requires that you understand what vocabulary your students have some knowledge of as they start your course. If you are teaching a higher level after an initial course, you can hopefully examine what topics and vocabulary the previous course covered, through the textbook, materials, tests, and so forth. You can also talk with teachers to learn what vocabulary strengths or weaknesses they observed in their former students. If you have any placement test results or interview notes, you can review those as well. Meeting your students for the first time in class is the time to get to know them. Tests and questionnaires are good ways to gather some useful information.

I have used and recommend the Vocabulary Levels Test (VLT) to estimate students' receptive vocabulary knowledge. The VLT assesses people's under-standing of words from the 1,000 to 2,000 word frequency bands of English (the 1,000 to 2,000 most frequent English words); the 3,000- and 5,000-word frequency levels; plus academic vocabulary. It does so using sets of six target words and asks test takers to match three of them with short defining words or phrases. This VLT is helpful for intermediate students, and, depending on their proficiency level, you may only choose to give them the test for a particular level (i.e., the 1,000- or 2,000-level test), because the others (e.g., the 4,000 to 5,000 levels) are simply beyond them. An example exists in the appendixes of Webb and Nation (2017), and different versions of the VLT vary slightly, with some starting with the 2,000-word level and including 10,000-word level and academic sections, while others start with the 1,000-word level, include a 4,000-word level, yet end at the 5,000-word level and do not include an academic section (as in Webb & Nation, 2017). Teachers can locate the version or section(s) best suited to their students and context.

Nation and his colleagues have created other options for beginning students. Two early versions of the 1,000 Word Level Test use statements and ask test takers to indicate if they are true or false. One item is "This is a square" (with a drawing of a square). Such versions can be photocopied and may be useful in ESL classes with students from different language back-grounds. A second option is to use a bilingual version of the 1,000-word-level test, particularly in EFL contexts where beginning students all have the same L1. It asks them to match sample target 1,000-level English vocabulary with words in their L1.

Yet another option is to use the Vocabulary Size Test (VST), which takes 10 sample items to test each of up to 20 levels representing knowledge of the 20,000 most frequent word families in English. More difficult than the VLT, the VST uses short English sentences and multiple-choice definitions, and is most suitable for intermediate through advanced students (for an online version, visit https://www.lextutor.ca/tests/vst). Various VST options are located at Paul Nation's web page, https://people.wgtn.ac.nz/paul.nation /publications. Several additional online vocabulary tests, including the VLT, are also available at https://www.lextutor.ca/tests.

REFLECTIVE QUESTIONS

- For your classes, what methods might you use to discern your students' vocabulary knowledge?

- Which of the tests outlined might you use? How?

- How might your students benefit from taking such a vocabulary test?

Diagnostic tests can help you determine your students' vocabulary knowledge and what vocabulary to focus on to meet their English learning objectives. Questionnaires can also help (see Figure 4.1 for a sample questionnaire).

Vocabulary Questionnaire

Why do you want to learn (more) English?

What do you currently do to learn English vocabulary?

Please give specific examples of places or situations where you need help to understand and communicate better in English:

What specific topics or kinds of vocabulary would you like to focus on learning in this course?

Figure 4.1. Sample of a student vocabulary questionnaire

My experience with questions like those in Figure 4.1 is that they prompt students to think about their learning goals, current practices, and particular contexts and subjects where I, as a teacher, might be able to help them to focus on vocabulary and vocabulary-learning strategies. When using this type of questionnaire with students, however, teachers must follow up on what they learn from it, ideally implementing what they learn about students in their teaching.

Step 2: Decide What Vocabulary to Focus on Teaching

After you use these options to see what your students' receptive vocabulary knowledge level is and what their goals are relative to your program or class, you can determine what vocabulary to focus on teaching them. If test results indicate that your students struggle with the 1,000– or 2,000–level words, then high-frequency words from those levels should be your priority. You might also choose to adopt a textbook that focuses on such words plus various points from this book to guide your teaching of this high-frequency vocabulary.

If, however, your students clearly know the high-frequency vocabulary quite well, then you will want to emphasize another level, say the 3,000– or the 5,000–word level from the VLT. This higher number reflects the mid-frequency vocabulary noted in chapter 2. If your students are also going to be taking college or university courses in English, then the academic vocabulary test is important to administer. You may want to adopt a coursebook that reviews high-frequency vocabulary but also introduces academic vocabulary items, or you might want to choose one that focuses primarily on academic vocabulary (see chapter 6 for the AVL and the NAWL). If results show that students need more mid-frequency vocabulary, then you might want to add a broad reading program or choose a text that focuses on it or even some discipline-specific terminology. The goal is helping students understand their vocabulary knowledge level and then showing them how the vocabulary they, their textbook, and your classes focus on will help them practice what they know and expand their vocabulary knowledge. Be sure to provide opportunities for productive vocabulary knowledge and use in class too.

REFLECTIVE QUESTION

- How might your textbook and other resources help students learn and practice the vocabulary you focus on?

Teaching Vocabulary

Chapter 5 introduces some technology and online resources that may be useful to you and your students as you incorporate and teach the right target vocabulary for your students.

Step 3: Teach Vocabulary and Follow Up

You need to focus your teaching on the learning and use of the appropriate vocabulary in the context of the listening, speaking, reading, and writing skills that students need to practice and develop. In this sense, you need to move beyond the macro (vocabulary size) to the micro (specific activities, topics, etc.) perspective. Do students need to learn and use vocabulary for shopping and their hobbies? For academic listening and reading, church, or sports? Are their vocabulary goals more receptive or productive? Drawing on the examples, teaching tips, and research-based perspectives throughout this book, you can teach English vocabulary and help students to understand and be able to use it to communicate effectively about topics and issues relevant to them.

Yet, teaching vocabulary is not yet complete at this point. You must follow up, both with your students and in terms of teaching. Ideally you should help monitor students' progress toward their vocabulary learning goals, as well as toward curricular ones. Are students reviewing vocabulary they have learned (using an app, their vocabulary notebooks, etc.)? Are they practicing the vocabulary learning strategies modeled in class? Are they learning to use the words and phrases being taught and focused on? To encourage greater depth of processing, you should ensure that students are learning to use new vocabulary in their speech and writing. You might have students bring their vocabulary cards or notebooks to class for peer review and teaching, and collect them afterward to offer students encouragement and suggestions through feedback on those valuable learning tools. If you value vocabulary and students' learning of it, then students will take vocabulary learning seriously!

You also need to monitor your vocabulary teaching. Are you spending sufficient time on the words and phrases you are targeting? Have you provided rich instruction incorporating vocabulary form, meaning, and use? At times, you can focus so much on the trees (individual vocabulary items) that you completely miss the forest (creating a supportive vocabulary learning environment). Review your lesson plans and ensure you devote adequate focus and time to vocabulary teaching, student learning, review, and practice, but you can also ask students for their feedback: What seems to be helpful for them to learn and practice new vocabulary? What else might be done to assist them, in class or during office hours? What apps or other resources will support students' vocabulary learning?

I recommend teachers occasionally use a *vocabulary minute paper* in class. I hand students a half-sheet of paper and give them 1 minute to focus on writing down something specific, such as all the new words they have learned that week, the vocabulary strategies they have been practicing, any questions they have about vocabulary, and so forth. This task enables me to follow up with students and target various aspects of vocabulary knowledge and learning. It also offers me some feedback on how I am doing in my vocabulary teaching. Usually, I do not grade these vocabulary minute papers but rather use them to provide students with some feedback.

REFLECTIVE QUESTIONS

- What question(s) might you ask your class to answer on their vocabulary minute papers?

- Write out one or two questions you can use for a vocabulary minute paper task in a specific course.

Step 4: Assess Your Teaching and Students' Vocabulary Learning

As you follow up in class, assess whether you need to adjust your vocabulary teaching in any way and be prepared to make adjustments to help students succeed. Perhaps the most objective measure of vocabulary teaching is to test students on a portion of what you have emphasized in class—words and phrases for specific topics, uses, and so forth. You must be careful to actually test what you have taught, however, and you should always consider any test results just one form of evidence of what students have learned. As an incremental process, vocabulary learning is best viewed over time. Results from midterms and final exams that test vocabulary are likely more accurate when complemented by students' vocabulary use in their coursework, to create a more holistic picture of students' vocabulary knowledge and use. Depending on your context, you may want to make vocabulary learning an explicit part of your course grades, which ensures some accountability to students and communicates that you take vocabulary teaching seriously.

REFLECTIVE QUESTIONS

- Think of one course you teach. What evidence might students see that you take vocabulary teaching seriously? If the evidence is not as clear as you would like, what change(s) might you make?

At the end of one course, I used a questionnaire on students' vocabulary-learning strategies and told them to list as many as 10 words they felt they had learned in class or elsewhere. The next week I gave each student one copy of a questionnaire, similar to the one in Figure 4.2, for each word they had listed. You might try this with one word from each student's vocabulary minute paper when you ask for new words they have recently learned. This type of assessment focuses on individual vocabulary learning, and it then provides both you and your students with feedback on their vocabulary learning. This task deals with form, meaning, and use, but also shows that grammatical knowledge is incorporated in vocabulary knowledge.

Vocabulary Knowledge Questionnaire

Word/phrase: _____

1. Please explain the meaning(s) for the word or phrase above:

2. Please use this word/phrase in a complete, correct English sentence:

3. Please check (✓) the word/phrase's part of speech (indicate all you know of):

_____ a noun—if yes, please indicate the plural form:

_____ a verb—if yes, please indicate the past tense:

_____ an adjective—if yes, please indicate the adverb form:

_____ an adverb—if yes, please indicate the adjective form:

Figure 4.2. Sample of a vocabulary knowledge questionnaire (adapted from Lessard-Clouston, 1996, p. 119)

With this type of questionnaire, you can grade each aspect—perhaps 2 points each for the definition and example sentence, but 1 point for the part of speech, for a total out of 5 (per word or phrase). If a student knows and lists more than one form (e.g., *joy* and *joyfully*), however, you might award bonus points. I like this kind of task because it reflects the things I ask students to include when they record a new vocabulary item on their word cards or in their notebooks.

REFLECTIVE QUESTION

- Based on your vocabulary teaching, what other information might you include in a vocabulary knowledge questionnaire? (e.g., pronunciation)

Conclusion

Coming to know students' vocabulary levels can assist teachers in deciding what vocabulary to focus on teaching, in monitoring their own teaching, in following up with students, and in providing a basis for assessing vocabulary teaching and students' learning. Knowing their students will also help teachers choose appropriate resources for vocabulary learning and teaching, to which we turn in the next two chapters.

Technology and Online Resources for Vocabulary Learning and Teaching

This chapter first summarizes findings concerning technology-mediated vocabulary development (TMVD). Next, it introduces several useful apps and online resources for English vocabulary learning and teaching that students and teachers can use in various contexts. The resources outlined here offer options for use in, outside of, and/or in conjunction with English classes to support vocabulary learning.

Technology-Mediated Vocabulary Development

In examining 82 research studies, Elgort (2018) concludes that TMVD "covers a wide range of instructional and learning treatments, contexts, and technologies" (p. 1), and that vocabulary development through technology can proceed with or without teacher involvement. Importantly, "studies comparing learning with and without technology reported a positive effect of TMVD much more often (96%) than studies that compared different technology-mediated learning approaches (46%)" (Elgort, 2018, p. 16). Teachers ideally support their students by helping them access and use the apps, websites, and other technologies valuable for learning English vocabulary in their context. Options to assist students' vocabulary learning include corpora and concordances, extensive reading materials, flash cards, games, lexical profilers, online dictionaries, and vocabulary tests, plus written and spoken input to support vocabulary learning through the skills of listening and speaking and reading and writing.

Research indicates the effectiveness of TMVD resources with different types of students. Utku and Dolgunsöz (2018) integrated online vocabulary games in Turkish fifth grade classes and conclude that they facilitated "EFL vocabulary learning and retention while they also provided a motivating learning atmosphere" (p. 124). Tsai (2019) used the Corpus of Contemporary American English (COCA) and a web-based dictionary with university EFL students to provide evidence that an inductive approach helps improve students' collocational knowledge, while a deductive one consolidates their definitional knowledge of recently learned words. Tsai also suggests that teachers use such tools to teach different aspects of vocabulary, like those outlined in chapter 1. Perhaps you could consider using Quizlet and/or WhatsApp.

Quizlet

Flash cards are a "very efficient method of learning the form-meaning connection of words" (Webb & Nation, 2017, p. 208). While some deeper processing may be involved when students create their own hard-copy word cards by writing words on one side and various types of information about them (e.g., a definition, translation, example sentence, and collocations) on the other side, several online software programs provide digital flash cards to review through an app. Quizlet is a popular one for ELLs and has several advantages when students use it to learn and review words. Quizlet allows students to hear and see words, for example, and it offers other vocabulary learning options besides just passively reviewing the form-meaning connection between words. Quizlet can be set up by the teacher for a class or for an individual student, or students can do so on their own, and the flash cards can be bilingual or only in English.

REFLECTIVE QUESTIONS

- Visit https://quizlet.com/. Determine how you might use it with one of your classes, to help students consolidate the form-meaning connection of words, learn how words are pronounced, and so on. Will you set it up or ask students to do so on their own? How can you connect its use to your class?

A number of my TESOL students use Quizlet effectively with their ESOL classes, including those for young learners and adult students. Quizlet includes flash cards for the Academic Vocabulary List, both English only and bilingual for seven languages, including Arabic, Chinese, Russian, and Spanish. Research using Quizlet successfully found that it not only increased vocabulary learning but also appeared to motivate students in their English studies. If Quizlet is not appropriate, then Anki, Flashcards+, or Memrise may be suitable.

WhatsApp

Among apps, WhatsApp is one of the most widely used in the world, which makes it ideal for many ESOL students and teachers to use both in and outside of their classes. WhatsApp allows individuals and groups to send different types of messages and to include texts, photos, audio files, and videos, so teachers can use it for vocabulary, homework, or other tasks where students practice their English vocabulary. Teachers use WhatsApp to encourage collaboration in their classes, extend learning time, and manage larger classes, as well as to flip their classes by having students watch videos or listen to audio in English before class that will then be discussed and used in class activities. Teachers can also provide feedback to students using WhatsApp in various formats, such as recorded messages, videos, and texts.

Research offers teachers encouragement for incorporating WhatsApp into their vocabulary teaching. Bensalem (2018) used WhatsApp with EFL students at a university in the Arabian Gulf to teach 20 new words per week for 6 weeks. Results indicate that the app was a positive learning tool that increased students' motivation for learning and that "using WhatsApp . . . significantly increased learners' vocabulary learning compared to the traditional method" (p. 32). Some teachers send a certain number of words each week to their students using WhatsApp, and have them focus on learning the meanings. They also answer questions about the target vocabulary using the app. As a result, they suggest that WhatsApp allows for more and greater comprehensible input for their students.

Teachers can search online for different ways that features of WhatsApp can be used with English classes, including for vocabulary, such as to address spelling, or to create audio diaries, a picture dictionary, or photo stories. One of my TESOL students reports that her ESL students use WhatsApp to share information and resources, enabling great authentic communication. She is encouraged that her students' creativity and personalities are evident through their use of WhatsApp for class and other tasks, offering a window into their lives and English learning, and helping them to motivate each other. WhatsApp has also been integrated with language goals to promote academic vocabulary learning in intensive English classes in the United States.

REFLECTIVE QUESTIONS

- What are several ways you could use WhatsApp to motivate your students and have them practice and use English vocabulary in relevant ways?

- How might you and your students use https://www.whatsapp.com/ to build on and enhance their classroom vocabulary learning?

While apps are available to students and teachers on their phones, web-based resources for vocabulary learning and teaching offer more options. I will introduce three.

The COCA

The Corpus of Contemporary American English (COCA), https://www .english-corpora.org/coca/, is accessible, web based, and freely available to teachers. A corpus is a large collection of texts, and the COCA focuses on spoken and written American English incorporating academic texts, fiction, newspapers, and popular magazines.

I cannot do justice to the COCA in an introduction; teachers must visit the website, explore it, and determine its helpfulness in their teaching. The five main COCA functions can help teachers determine which words and phrases to focus on in class and how to go about it. "List" helps locate single words or phrases in the 1-billion-word COCA, or search for synonyms or their use in wordlists. "Chart" locates words and their total frequency for particular genres (e.g., spoken, fiction, newspapers) or time periods. "Collocates" deals with collocations and determines which words appear before or after other particular items, offering information on their meaning and usage. More specifically, "Compare" offers information for comparing two sets of collocates, to understand how two words differ in meaning and use. Finally, the "Key Word in Context" (KWIC) function allows users to see words with up to three words to the left (before) and/or right of (behind) it, which is valuable for examining grammatical and other patterns of specific words. Other options now include "Word" for accessing detailed information about specific vocabulary items and their use in the corpus, and "Browse" to learn about numerous types of information and see examples of specific words or phrases in the COCA.

Teachers can sign up for an account and will then be eligible to create and save their own virtual corpus drawn from the COCA for future use. While the COCA is worth bookmarking for quick searches, as outlined here, various online videos introduce other specific ways the COCA can give detailed information on English vocabulary use for particular words and phrases over time. The English corpora site also provides useful options under the "Related Resources" tab, including WordAndPhrase and Academic Vocabulary Lists. My TESOL students use the COCA to check for vocabulary use and phrasing when writing academic papers, to find real-life spoken or written examples incorporating vocabulary they highlight in their teaching, and to research examples and the number of occurrences of words they want ESOL students to notice, study, and understand. The COCA is also excellent to consult when a student asks whether to use one or more particular English words or word forms (e.g., *geographic* vs. *geographical*)!

Lee, Warschauer, and Lee (2019) surveyed 29 different studies involving corpora for vocabulary learning and conclude that "the overall effect of corpus use on L2 vocabulary learning" is positive, with the greatest benefits for students with at least intermediate-level proficiency (p. 745). They note that using corpora is more effective when concordance lines are selected for students and accompanied by "hands-on corpus-use opportunities" (p. 745), supporting teachers using data-driven learning.

REFLECTIVE QUESTIONS

- Visit and explore https://www.english-corpora.org/coca/. Which of the five main functions do you see yourself using for your classes? How might you incorporate it for a whole class or with a smaller group of students?

- For what other possibilities mentioned here might you use the COCA to support your vocabulary teaching? Students' vocabulary learning?

Compleat Lexical Tutor

Another amazing website too complex to detail here is the Compleat Lexical Tutor, which incorporates many resources for teachers and students, including concordancers, flash cards, graded readers, a quick look-up or listen search for American and British English, word games, and vocabulary tests. Like the COCA, Lextutor is an expanding and often updated site, so I cannot do it justice in a short introduction. Instead, I encourage teachers to invest time to explore this free site, including the research base for the various components. Note, however, that a number of aspects of the website, including cloze, flash cards, morpholex, and tests, are also available in mobile format through the Lextutor app.

REFLECTIVE QUESTIONS

- Explore https://www.lextutor.ca/, noting 2 to 3 options that you could use with your classes. Might you want students to use the app? Why (not)?

VocabProfilers

One valuable resource on the Lextutor site that every teacher should know about is VocabProfilers (VP). VP offers lexical profiles by matching the vocabulary within a text to corpus-based vocabulary lists (such as those noted in chapter 6) using a web-based program. Teachers can copy and paste a reading or listening passage into the main text box, choose the option(s) desired, and then click submit. The program then provides an output list that first indicates how much vocabulary is found on particular lists, and second provides color-coded lists so that teachers can see the specific words from the passage on those lists, at the various levels.

VocabProfilers is important because one of the most robust findings from English vocabulary research is that students usually need adequate comprehension of some 95% to 98% of the words in a passage to be able to learn new words from it (Barclay & Schmitt, 2019). This means ideally no more than 1 in 20 to 50 words are unknown to listeners or readers. VocabProfilers helps teachers see how many words are high frequency and academic, and how many are "off list," meaning they are not on any of the particular lists chosen for the analysis. As a result, teachers can identify the level of difficulty of a listening or reading passage, as well as any challenging vocabulary in it that may need to be explained, glossed, or taught explicitly before students read or listen to it.

There are now several VocabProfilers (VP). VP-kids supports first and second language development for grades 0 to 3; VP-Classic (the original version) is now geared toward grades 4 to 8, with the Middle School Subject Lists as one corpus option; and VP-Compleat supports language development from grade 9 through college or university. VP-Compleat allows users to select from a number of different corpus options, including the British National Corpus (BNC), the BNC-COCA 25, the Common European Framework of Reference for Languages (CEFR-English) list, and the NGSL+NAWL (see chapter 6 for details). The newest addition is VP-COCA, which offers single word frequencies in texts. Teachers who use one of these VocabProfilers to examine the vocabulary in a listening or reading passage will be able to determine if the text is appropriate for their students and, if not, either to select a different passage or to adapt the text to make it more suitable. One way to do so can be to replace very low-frequency words that appear only once with other, better-known words to simplify the text slightly and help improve its comprehensibility for students.

English writing teachers might have their high-intermediate or advanced students use VP-Compleat by asking them to copy and paste their essays into the program (after having learned how to use it!) and run the analysis. Particularly for English for Academic Purposes (EAP), such a task helps students to learn how academic their writing is, and whether they are using an appropriate mix of high-frequency, academic, and low-frequency vocabulary.

Conclusion

This chapter introduced research on technology-mediated vocabulary development, as well as several apps and internet resources for teaching vocabulary and to support student learning. As all such resources change over time, teachers will need to keep up to date, however!

CHAPTER 6

Using Word Lists in Vocabulary Teaching: Options and Possibilities

As English has one of the largest vocabularies, "the lexical challenge facing learners, both in terms of single items and formulaic sequences, is considerable" (Barclay & Schmitt, 2019, p. 5). Accordingly, deciding what words to teach is of primary concern to teachers. As previously indicated, corpus linguistics offers helpful resources, and word lists are great examples. This chapter introduces options and possibilities for using English word lists in vocabulary teaching.

Early English Word Lists

The most well-known principled English word list is West's (1953) General Service List (GSL), representing the 2,000 most frequent words, divided into the first- and second-thousand words in the language. Like most word lists, the GSL focuses on objective criteria, word frequency and range, while incorporating some subjective perspectives. Widely available online, the GSL is still used in ESOL materials, but as an old list created before computers, it has issues and has been replaced by two better and more up-to-date New General Service Lists introduced here and summarized in Table 6.1.

Coxhead's (2000) Academic Word List (AWL) is built upon the GSL and offers ESL students 570 frequent words that are particularly useful in reading academic texts. The AWL assumes students know GSL vocabulary and is divided into 10 sublists that reflect English frequency and range in the arts, commerce, law, and science. Also widely available, the AWL is incorporated into many textbooks and materials, and remains an important resource for EAP.

REFLECTIVE QUESTIONS

- What is your experience with the GSL and/or the AWL? Do your teaching materials acknowledge or incorporate them? If you are familiar with these lists, what advantages or challenges have you noted with them?

Current General English Word Lists

Researchers in Europe and Japan updated the GSL with new versions, creating the new-GSL (Brezina & Gablasova, 2015) and the NGSL (Browne, 2014) respectively. Improvements involved significantly larger corpora, an effort to incorporate updated sources reflecting both American and British English, and a focus on results that recognize the needs of English language learners. The new-GSL uses a corpus of 12.1 billion words, virtually all of which were written, much of which was drawn from the internet. The NGSL is based on a 274-million-word subset of the Cambridge English Corpus, but includes one-quarter spoken and three-quarters written English. Both lists have dedicated websites and are beginning to appear in English teaching materials. Noteworthy is that these newer general English lists are longer than the GSL: the NGSL has about 2,800 words and the new-GSL approximately 2,500 words.

Most recently, Dang and Webb (2016) published an Essential Word List (EWL) for beginning English language learners, recognizing that teachers and students in EFL contexts need a more manageable list of words than those longer general lists. The EWL is based on a 136-million-word (19% spoken, 81% written) corpus that draws from 10 varieties of English, and so it is very international. The EWL was particularly created for students who are just learning the first 1,000 words and whose English morphology knowledge may not enable them to recognize English words at higher levels of English frequency (Dang, 2020). Divided into 176 very frequent function words and 624 lexical items, the EWL is also helpfully arranged into 13 sublists based on frequency and coverage in spoken and written English.

REFLECTIVE QUESTIONS

- In your teaching context, which general English word list seems most appropriate? Consider your students, the importance of written versus spoken English input, the size of the lists, and relevant materials available.

Current Academic English Word Lists

Newer academic English lists to know about are the Academic Vocabulary List (AVL) and the New Academic Word List (NAWL).

Uniquely, the AVL does not assume knowledge of the GSL, but instead offers the 3,015 most frequent and wide-ranging words in a much larger and more diverse academic corpus than the AWL (Gardner & Davies, 2014). For EAP, I encourage my TESOL students to use the AVL as a replacement for both the GSL and the AWL, because it offers a clearer focus. In addition, the AVL is further subdivided into nine important disciplines relevant to those working in EAP: education, humanities, history, social sciences, philosophy/religion/psychology, law/political science, science and technology, medicine/health, and business/finance. A dedicated academic vocabulary website has further options, drawing upon the AVL (see Table 6.1). A number of resources incorporate the AVL, such as Quizlet, noted in chapter 5.

Also for EAP, the NAWL was created using a 288-million-word corpus that drew from an academic subset of the Cambridge English Corpus (86.3%), plus thousands of English textbooks (12.6%), and 3 million words (1.1%) from the Michigan Corpus of Academic Spoken English (MICASE) and the British Academic Spoken English (BASE) corpus. Used together, the 960-word NAWL and the NGSL provide 92% coverage of the academic corpus, about 5% better coverage than the combined GSL and AWL (87%) for the same corpus (Browne, Culligan, & Phillips, n.d.). While both the AVL and the NAWL are available for Quizlet and Memrise apps, I am not yet aware of any textbooks that focus on teaching these EAP lists.

The unit for counting words is important to consider with word lists. The two main approaches are "lemmas" and "flemmas." A "lemma" is simply a word (*form*) along with its inflections (*forms, formed, forming*), but all the members are the same word class. As Dang (2020) explains, "The flemma is similar to the lemma, but it does not distinguish parts of speech" (p. 290). As an example, when *form* is a noun and a verb, it counts as two lemmas, but just one flemma. The unit of counting is included in Table 6.1, which summarizes recent and important word list options for English vocabulary teaching—three general and two academic.

Table 6.1. Important Word Lists for Vocabulary Teaching

List/Source	Focus, Purpose, and Additional Information	Comments
Essential Word List (EWL) (Dang & Webb, 2016)	An 800-word list for beginners: 176 function words (*the, and, of*) and 624 lexical words (*know, like, well, just, think*), further divided into 13 sublists, according to frequency and coverage in 9 spoken and 9 written corpora representing 10 varieties of English. Addresses practicality and uses flemmas. Available at https://www.edu.uwo.ca/faculty -profiles/docs/other/webb/essential-word-list.pdf.	A great, short list for EFL beginners. Note overlap with new- GSL, etc.
New General Service List (NGSL) (Browne, 2014)	A list of 2,818 general English flemmas reflecting the most frequent words within a 273.6-million- word subset of the Cambridge English Corpus. The focus is English language learners' needs. This list provides 92.34% coverage of the corpus and was developed following updated criteria from West (1953). The list and details are available at *http://www.newgeneralservicelist.org/*.	Based on spoken (25%) and written (75%) American and British English.

continued on next page

Table 6.1. Important Word Lists for Vocabulary Teaching *(continued)*

List/Source	Focus, Purpose, and Additional Information	Comments
New General Service List (new-GSL) (Brezina & Gablasova, 2015)	A list of 2,494 general English lemmas, reflecting the most frequent words in a collection of four corpora, which represent 12.1 billion words, based on analyses of three quantitative measures: frequency, dispersion, and distribution across the corpora. Coverage of the list in the four corpora is 80.1% to 81.7%. The list is available as Supplementary Data at https://academic.oup.com /applij/article/36/1/1/226623. For further details, see also http://corpora.lancs.ac.uk/vocab/.	Based on written (99.92%) English. Most suited to British English?
Academic Vocabulary List (AVL) (Gardner & Davies, 2014)	A list of 3,015 lemmas distinguished by part of speech, representing the most frequent words in the 120-million-word academic subcorpus of the COCA. Prepared for EAP, the AVL represents about 14% of the academic materials in the COCA and the BNC. The AVL is further subdivided into nine important disciplines. See details at http://www.academicvocabulary.info/.	A newer alternative to the GSL plus the AWL.
New Academic Word List (NAWL) (Browne, Culligan, & Phillips, n.d.)	Also for EAP, the 960-word NAWL uses English flemmas and was created from a 288-million-word academic corpus of academic discourse, academic journals, essays, and textbooks, along with 3 million spoken words from the MICASE and the BASE corpora. Meant to be combined with the NGSL. Available at http://www.newgeneralservicelist.org /nawl-new-academic-word-list.	Reflects mainly written American and British English.

REFLECTIVE QUESTIONS

- Given your context and the classes you teach, which word list(s) in Table 6.1 should you make your students aware of? Why? How might you use them?

- For general English, should you perhaps focus on teaching the EWL, the NGSL, or the new-GSL? For EAP, why might you choose the AVL or NAWL?

- Visit the websites listed for the lists of interest to you to learn more.

Possibilities for Word Lists in the Classroom

A word list can help set short- or long-term vocabulary learning goals for students and assist teachers with course design, in addition to helping focus teachers and learners on target vocabulary in activities, materials, and even quizzes and tests in classes. For example, a beginning EFL course might be created around the EWL, and once students master that, they could move on to the NGSL. Intermediate courses could focus on the NGSL or the new-GSL. Students studying EAP should perhaps learn the AVL, or the NGSL and then the NAWL.

Lessard-Clouston (2012/2013) introduces older lists plus a number of specialized ones for business, engineering, science, and theology, as well as practical suggestions for using word lists with students. The AWL and EWL sublists, for example, provide smaller word sets for teaching and student learning, perhaps using an app or word cards. A growing number of text-books use principled word lists, and adopting one relevant to your context provides a curriculum to support students' learning of the chosen list. Input in the form of reading passages or TED talks that incorporate target word list vocabulary is ideal and can provide content for student output tasks involving speaking and writing practicing target words. The possibilities are limited only by teachers' creativity once they choose the list most relevant to their students.

Additional Important Word Lists

The important lists in Table 6.1 deal with individual words. Yet, as noted earlier, multiword items are important for helping students develop fluency in their comprehension and production in English. To help students develop the collocational knowledge that Nation (2020) highlights, for example, Shin and Nation's (2008) 100 most frequent collocations in spoken English from the BNC offer an excellent list to incorporate into speaking and listening courses. Other possible lists include Martinez and Schmitt's (2012) Phrasal Expressions List of 505 multiword expressions and Garnier and Schmitt's (2015) PHaVE list of 150 phrasal verbs from the COCA, which are practical and help note different senses of these formulaic expressions, which can be incorporated into various types of English classes for students with different proficiency levels, interests, and English language needs. For EAP, the Academic Spoken Word List is yet another option for helping students comprehend academic speech in English-medium lectures and campus situations. Finally, for middle and high school EAP, the Middle School Vocabulary Lists and Secondary School Vocabulary Lists are worthy of attention—check them out online.

REFLECTIVE QUESTIONS

- What possibilities come to mind for using a particular word list in your course? What creative ways will you incorporate such vocabulary in class?

- Are any of the additional word lists mentioned of special interest? Check the References and locate them for more information for your classes.

Conclusion

This chapter has introduced the newest, most important corpus-based English word lists for English language teachers and their students.

Putting It Together: Vocabulary Teaching Guidelines

Although individual students' goals may differ, in English "a large vocabulary is required for language use" (Schmitt, 2010, p. 6). Various authors argue, for example, that sound knowledge of 4,000 to 5,000 word families is required for intermediate-level performance, with at least 6,000 to 9,000 for advanced proficiency. Teachers, then, should help students learn as much vocabulary as possible and as much about each item as required for its productive use (see Table 1.1). This chapter aims to put it all together by summarizing several approaches that offer clear guidelines for incorporating vocabulary into an ESOL course.

Use Nation's Four Strands for Teaching Vocabulary

Nation (2013) suggests using four equal strands in language teaching. For vocabulary these involve

1. meaning-focused *input* for listening and reading practice, particularly with graded readers;

2. meaning-focused *output* for speaking and writing;

3. *deliberate teaching*, using rich vocabulary instruction, raising students' word consciousness, and modeling vocabulary learning strategies; and

4. developing *fluency* with vocabulary across language skills (by emphasizing practice and helping to make connections with already known vocabulary).

Learners' main role, according to Webb and Nation (2017), is to take active responsibility for their vocabulary learning by 1) deliberately learning words both in and out of the classroom, 2) encountering the target vocabulary outside of class, and 3) using vocabulary (i.e., to practice). In contrast, the teacher's main jobs involve planning lessons that incorporate these four strands, training students to use vocabulary-learning strategies, testing their vocabulary knowledge and use (and interpreting the results), and teaching vocabulary in a principled fashion. I welcome this division because it helps teachers understand their roles and gives them a clear plan to accomplish their teaching objectives and also enables learners to understand and take responsibility for their own learning in and out of class.

REFLECTIVE QUESTIONS

● Please read Vignette 2 and then answer the questions.

Vignette 2: Vocabulary Learning

Hendro takes EFL courses in academic writing and TOEFL preparation as an undergraduate business administration student at a university in Indonesia. Some of his courses use English language textbooks or case studies, although his professors and fellow students usually discuss and write about them in Indonesian. Next semester, a British lecturer is coming as a visiting scholar to his school, and Hendro plans to take her business course taught in English. After graduation, he hopes to complete an international master's of business administration degree program in an English-speaking country and return to Indonesia to work with a multinational company. Hendro is comfortable reading in English but struggles with specialized vocabulary. He is also concerned about whether he will be able to follow the visiting professor's lectures and give presentations in her class. He plans to buy some resources to study English during the break.

— What suggestions would you give Hendro on resources to buy or use to help him learn vocabulary? How might you recommend he fulfill his learner role according to Webb and Nation's approach?

— As Hendro's EFL teacher, how might you structure his classes to address Nation's four strands effectively? What vocabulary would you emphasize? What principles, strategies, and assessments might you use?

Adopt Zimmerman's Word-Consciousness Approach

Zimmerman (2009) argues that *word consciousness* is key in vocabulary teaching, because it is an "alertness to words" (p. 3). She suggests that features to consider include register, precision, word choices in speech and writing, collocation, and word formation. For particular courses, Zimmerman (2009) offers the following guidelines for vocabulary teaching.

First, teachers should "be selective about the words you target" in their lessons, by explaining, recycling, and practicing appropriate words based on frequency, salience, learners' goals, and the learning burden of words (Zimmerman, 2009, pp. 7–8). They cannot teach every word, but they can choose those most suited to their students' vocabulary needs. Second, teachers should "be selective about the information you present," by preteaching words briefly based on the information relevant to particular activities and notice their students' vocabulary errors (p. 9). Third, teachers should "provide adequate repetition," with 10 or more encounters with new words, spacing these and using various types of tasks in class for their introduction, instruction, and repetition (pp. 9–10). Fourth, teachers should offer "effective vocabulary practice" by structuring their lessons carefully (e.g., use familiar vocabulary, repeat themes, and sequence practice), using "interesting and relevant contexts," and making them meaningful, interactive, and focused by practicing functions, using teachable moments, and facilitating "student-centered group work" (pp. 11–12). Fifth, teachers should "monitor students' understanding" and learning through regular feedback (p. 12).

I appreciate Zimmerman's (2009) approach to vocabulary teaching because it is rational and realistic yet also assumes and builds on an incremental perspective on vocabulary learning (reflected in Table 3.1). Like Nation's (2013) four strands, Zimmerman's word-consciousness guidelines work particularly well after getting to know students and their vocabulary needs, as discussed in chapter 4. I recommend my TESOL students use Nation's four-strands approach to frame the vocabulary component of their ESOL courses and also adapt Zimmerman's (2009) guidelines in the actual pedagogy of teaching specific vocabulary in their individual lessons.

REFLECTIVE QUESTIONS

- Think of a particular lesson you teach. Use Zimmerman's guidelines to focus your vocabulary teaching.

- Determine which items to teach, what information to offer about each, and how to incorporate enough exposures.

- Enable students to practice this vocabulary.

- Monitor student learning and offer feedback.

As much as possible, ESOL educators should teach their students to learn and use words and phrases in context, so they should normally use and give example sentences in both spoken and written form. As Zimmerman suggests, teachers should also actively teach the meaning of specific words, using various materials, strategies, and techniques appropriate to their students and contexts. One potential way to do so is to use specific themes in teaching vocabulary, using various types of readings to help English language learners develop their general, academic, and other vocabulary knowledge in relevant content areas.

Incorporate Multiword Expressions Into Vocabulary Teaching

As noted in chapter 1, vocabulary includes multiword units, also called formulaic sequences and lexical chunks or phrases, and teachers should incorporate them into vocabulary teaching. There are different kinds of lexical chunks, including core idioms (*to pull someone's leg*), figuratives (*to toe the line*), and literal sequences (*at the moment*) (Nation, 2013).

The first two cannot normally be understood just by looking at the parts of the expression alone, but literal sequences can often be comprehended by considering the meaning of the parts, especially if students' native languages use similar equivalents. Zimmerman (2009) also includes phrasal verbs (*to turn on*) and notes that idioms can be more or less fixed (*to kick the bucket*) or variable (*from head to foot*, but also *from head to toe*). If teachers provide example sentences for students as they introduce and teach vocabulary, then these types of multiword expressions will naturally appear quite regularly, and students will see them in context. Highlight them by underlining them on the board, and perhaps pointing out whether they are fixed or variable.

Multiword expressions represent a promising area of research on teaching English. As chapter 6 noted, Shin and Nation (2008) published a list of the 100 most frequent collocations in spoken English in the BNC, including *you know* (#1), *I think* (#2), and *thank you* (#8). Similarly, Martinez and Schmitt (2012) published a Phrasal Expressions List (PHRASE List) of "the 505 most frequent non-transparent multiword expressions in English," based on the BNC (p. 299). Their top three are *have to*, *there is/are*, and *such as* (p. 307). Garnier and Schmitt's (2015) PHaVE list includes 150 phrasal verbs from the COCA and indicates different senses. Vocabulary from all three lists can easily be incorporated into English language classes.

These lists may be used along with others discussed in chapter 6. Alali and Schmitt (2012) studied teaching multiword expressions and confirm that "at least some of the same types of teaching methodologies we use for individual words can be effective in teaching formulaic sequences" (p. 174). They argue that reviewing words and phrases is necessary, because "learners need to engage with words numerous times in order to learn them" (p. 169).

REFLECTIVE QUESTIONS

- What ways do you highlight multiword expressions in your teaching?

- What additional methods might you use to incorporate them?

Use Corpora to Inform Vocabulary Teaching and Learning

As demonstrated in this book, much useful information, including English word-frequency counts, collocation information, and important lists, is available to teachers because of corpus linguistics research. Where possible, English language teachers should use corpora to inform their teaching, choice of materials, and students' learning. Frequency views of vocabulary require corpus-based research, and corpus evidence for vocabulary learning and teaching is usually more effective than intuition. Chapters 5 and 6 introduced corpora and corpus-informed resources.

REFLECTIVE QUESTIONS

- What advantages do you see with a data-driven learning approach to vocabulary teaching based on corpora? Any challenges?

- Visit https://www.lextutor.ca/research/ to see the rationale behind that site, plus research papers and presentations of potential interest.

Conclusion

The task of vocabulary teaching is enormous. This chapter offered further ways to teach English words and phrases, with guidelines for teaching vocabulary in ESOL classes. With the research base highlighted in Webb's (2020) handbook and an open access journal entitled *Vocabulary Learning and Instruction*, http://vli-journal.org/, the future for vocabulary teaching has never looked brighter.

In sum, this short book has defined vocabulary and introduced its importance in language learning and teaching. It has provided an L2 perspective on understanding vocabulary and given a brief outline of research-based tips for vocabulary teaching. It has also summarized how to identify students' vocabulary knowledge and needs, introduced various online resources and word lists, and noted how to put all of this information into action using relevant vocabulary teaching guidelines. The reflection questions and tasks help you apply all this to your teaching situation, and additional resources are offered in the References. As a bonus, a sample vocabulary teaching lesson plan, which incorporates a number of topics introduced here, such as word families, word parts, focusing on form, meaning, and use, as well as incorporating technology and dictionary use, is included as an appendix. All the best in teaching vocabulary!

REFLECTIVE QUESTIONS

- What examples or guidelines outlined seem most useful to help you integrate vocabulary teaching into your classes?

- What action steps should you now take to implement these?

References

Alali, F. A., & Schmitt, N. (2012). Teaching formulaic sequences: The same as or different from teaching single words? *TESOL Journal, 3*(2), 153–180. https://doi.org/10.1002/tesj.13

Barclay, S., & Schmitt, N. (2019). Current perspectives on vocabulary teaching and learning. In X. Gao (Ed.), *Second handbook of English language teaching* (pp. 1–22). Springer. https://doi.org/10.1007/978-3-319-58542-0_42-1

Barker, D. (2007). A personalized approach to analyzing 'cost' and 'benefit' in vocabulary selection. *System, 35*(4), 523–533. https://doi.org/10.1016/j.system.2007.09.001

Bensalem, E. (2018). The impact of WhatsApp on EFL students' vocabulary learning. *Arab World English Journal, 9*(1), 23–38. https://doi.org/10.24093/awej/vol9no1.2

Brezina, V., & Gablasova, D. (2015). Is there a core general vocabulary? Introducing the *New General Service List. Applied Linguistics, 36*(1), 1–22. https://doi.org/10.1093/applin/amt018

Brown, D. (2011). What aspects of vocabulary knowledge do textbooks give attention to? *Language Teaching Research, 15*(1), 83–97. https://doi.org/10.1177/1362168810383345

Browne, C. (2014). A New General Service List: The better mousetrap we've been looking for? *Vocabulary Learning and Instruction, 3*(2), 1–10. https://doi.org/10.7820/vli.v03.2.browne

Browne, C., Culligan, B., & Phillips, J. (n.d.). A new academic word list. Retrieved from http://www.newgeneralservicelist.org/nawl-new-academic-word-list/.

Coxhead, A. (2000). A new academic word list. *TESOL Quarterly, 34*(2), 213–238. https://doi.org/10.5054/tq.2011.254528

Dang, T. N. Y. (2020). Corpus-based word lists in second language vocabulary research, learning, and teaching. In S. Webb (Ed.), *The Routledge handbook of vocabulary studies* (pp. 288–303). Routledge.

Dang, T. N. Y., & Webb, S. (2016). Making an essential word list for beginners. In P. Nation, *Making and using word lists for language learning and testing* (pp. 153–167). Benjamins.

Elgort, I. (2018). Technology-mediated second language vocabulary development: A review of trends in research methodology. *CALICO Journal, 35*(1), 1–29. https://doi.org/10.1558/cj.34554

Folse, K. (2011). Applying L2 lexical research findings in ESL teaching. *TESOL Quarterly, 45*(2), 362–369. https://doi.org/10.5054/tq.2010.254529

Gardner, D., & Davies, M. (2014). A new academic vocabulary list. *Applied Linguistics, 35*(3), 305–327. https://doi.org/10.1093/applin/amt015

Garnier, M., & Schmitt, N. (2015). The PHaVE list: A pedagogical list of phrasal verbs and their most frequent meaning senses. *Language Teaching Research, 19*(6), 645–666. https://doi.org/10.1177/1362168814559798

Horst, M. (2019). *Focus on vocabulary learning*. Oxford University Press.

Lee, H., Warschauer, M., & Lee, J. H. (2019). The effects of corpus use on second language vocabulary learning: A multilevel meta-analysis. *Applied Linguistics, 40*(5), 721–753. https://doi.org/10.1093/applin/amy012

Lessard-Clouston, M. (1996). ESL vocabulary learning in a TOEFL preparation class: A case study. *Canadian Modern Language Review, 53*(1), 97–119. https://doi.org/10.3138/cmlr.53.1.97

Lessard-Clouston, M. (2010). Theology lectures as lexical environments: A case study of technical vocabulary use. *Journal of English for Academic Purposes, 9*(4), 308–321. https://doi.org/10.1016/j.jeap.2010.09.001

Lessard-Clouston, M. (2012/2013). Word lists for vocabulary learning and teaching. *The CATESOL Journal, 24*(1), 287–304.

Lewis, M. (1993). *The lexical approach: The state of ELT and a way forward*. Language Teaching Publications.

McCrostie, J. (2007). Investigating the accuracy of teachers' word frequency intuitions. *RELC Journal, 38*(1), 53–66. https://doi.org/10.1177/0033688206076158

Martinez, R., & Schmitt, N. (2012). A phrasal expressions list. *Applied Linguistics, 33*(3), 299–320. https://doi.org/10.1093/applin/ams010

Nation, I. S. P. (2013). *Learning vocabulary in another language* (2nd ed.). Cambridge University Press.

Nation, P. (2020). The different aspects of vocabulary knowledge. In S. Webb (Ed.), *The Routledge handbook of vocabulary studies* (pp. 15–29). Routledge.

O'Loughlin, R. (2012). Tuning in to vocabulary frequency in coursebooks. *RELC Journal, 43*(2), 255–269. https://doi.org/10.1177/0033688212450640

Schmitt, N. (2010). *Researching vocabulary: A vocabulary research manual*. Palgrave Macmillan.

Schmitt, N., & Schmitt, D. (2014). A reassessment of frequency and vocabulary size in L2 teaching. *Language Teaching, 47*(4), 484–503. https://doi.org/10.1017 /S0261444812000018

Shin, D., & Nation, P. (2008). Beyond single words: The most frequent collocations in spoken English. *ELT Journal, 62*(4), 339–348. https://doi.org/10.1093/elt/ccm091

Tsai, K.-J. (2019). Corpora and dictionaries as learning aids: Inductive versus deductive approaches to constructing vocabulary knowledge. *Computer Assisted Language Learning, 32*(8), 805–826. https://doi.org/10/1080/09588221.2018.1527366

Ur, P. (2012). *Vocabulary activities*. Cambridge University Press.

Utku, Ö., & Dolgunsöz, E. (2018). Teaching EFL vocabulary to young digital natives through online games: A study with Turkish 5th grade EFL learners. *International Online Journal of Education and Teaching, 5*(1), 115–130.

Webb, S. (Ed.). (2020). *The Routledge handbook of vocabulary studies*. Routledge.

Webb, S., & Nation, P. (2017). *How vocabulary is learned*. Oxford University Press.

West, M. (1953). *A general service list of English words*. Longman, Green, & Company.

Wilkins, D. (1972). *Linguistics in language teaching*. Arnold.

Zimmerman, C. B. (2009). *Word knowledge: A vocabulary teacher's handbook*. Oxford University Press.

Appendix: Sample Vocabulary Teaching Lesson Plan on Family

Background Information

This stand-alone, 1-hour lesson plan is meant to supplement a unit on *family*, a common topic in ESOL textbooks. It is geared toward an intermediate-level ESL class at a community college in North America that consists of 15 to 20 students, aged 18 to 60, who have various L1 backgrounds.

Rationale

As Nation (2013) argues, input, output, deliberate teaching, and fluency development are key to vocabulary learning. These activities aim to build on those in textbooks but include opportunities for each of these things, mainly to help students review and develop fluency with newer words and phrases, as well as those they already know. I believe a whole-class focus, as well as pair work, has a place and that allowing students to make choices about key vocabulary for them is useful, as is having students use online dictionaries, understand word families, and word parts.

Textbook *family* word lists tend to focus on very frequent words such as aunt, brother, cousin, daughter, father, niece, uncle, and wife, and so on.

These activities can help students develop fluency with those, but also assist them in learning new *family* vocabulary. I encourage students to use full sentences when possible, especially in pair work practice, and to check the form, meaning, and use of their new or previously known English vocabulary in this lesson's activities.

Overall Lesson Plan Objectives

- Review and expand student vocabulary related to *family* through explicit study of word families, dictionary use, and vocabulary review.
- Students develop understanding of form, meaning, and use of target vocabulary.
- Develop students' speaking fluency through contextualized communicative practice.

1. Warm-up

    a. *Objectives*

        — activate background knowledge

        — generate vocabulary students know

    b. *Time:* 10 minutes

    c. *Interaction:* teacher-students; student pairs; debrief

    d. *Materials:* projector, classroom computer, internet access, students' phones/devices with internet access, preset survey question on www.polleverywhere.com

    e. *Procedures*

        1. Teacher (T) asks students (Ss): *What family situations do you have experience with?*

        2. T calls on 2 Ss and asks them to briefly share about their family situations.

        3. T sets the next task: *What **different** family situations are you familiar with?*

        4. Pairs of Ss list family possibilities (e.g., adoption, extended families, single parents, etc.).

        5. T directs Ss to a preset survey question on www.polleverywhere.com that is sent at the beginning of class through WhatsApp.

6. Ss type their responses (one word or short phrases) and the answers are turned into a word cloud in the survey, displayed in class for everyone to see.

7. T reviews the posted words and makes a mental note about what vocabulary students already know (and any possible spelling mistakes, etc., to be addressed later).

8. Using the student-generated word cloud, T debriefs about various family situations (e.g., nuclear and extended families, blended families, divorce, engaged couples, etc.).

2. Expanding Vocabulary Through Word Parts, Dictionary Use, and Sentence-Level Practice

a. *Objectives*

— Ss learn about (and how to expand their vocabulary through) word families

— Ss practice using an online dictionary to find word families, noting word parts

— Ss focus on form, meaning, and use in writing sentences with new words

b. *Time:* 20 minutes

c. *Interaction:* T → Ss; pair work; Ss write individually; debrief

d. *Materials:* student phones/devices with internet access; projector and classroom computer with internet access; student handout (H/O) #1 (Family Vocabulary), sections 1. a. and b.

e. *Procedures*

1. T gives Ss H/O #1 and introduces the task: *We are going to see if these family-related words have different parts of speech. When we know one new word, we can learn several new words from the same word family. Some dictionaries provide such word families.*

2. T briefly models how to use an online dictionary. Students get a link to use the dictionary on their phones/devices. I chose https://www.ldoceonline.com because it displays word families at the top of the entries for these words, noting different parts of speech.

3. Ss work in pairs to complete the 1.a. chart with different part of speech possibilities.

Noun	Adjective	Adverb	Verb
adoption/adoptee/adopter	adopted	XXXXX	**to adopt**
brother	brotherly	XXXXX	XXXXX
divorce/divorcé(e)	**divorced**	XXXXX	to divorce
(re)marriage	(re)**married**	XXXXX	to (re)marry
relative/relation(ship)	(un)related	**Relatively**	to relate

4. T asks pairs to share their findings from the online dictionary, noting that most of these family related words do <u>not</u> have an adverb form. If time allows, T points out related words formed with affixes, such as *re-*, *un-*, and *-ship*, noting their meaning and stating these are key word parts. T may ask Ss if they know any other words that incorporate these affixes.

5. Ss work individually to complete exercise 1.b. T then asks 1 student to share an example sentence for each of the 5 words, commenting on form, meaning, and use.

3. Communicative Practice—Vocabulary Pair Review

a. *Objectives*

— Ss choose and focus on reviewing family-related vocabulary with a partner

— Ss define 9 words/phrases, or make notes to help them explain the target items

b. *Time:* 15 minutes

c. *Interaction:* T explanation; pair work; class debrief

d. *Materials:* H/O #1, part 2.

e. *Procedures*

1. T explains that there are 16 family-related words or phrases in part 2. of H/O #1, and briefly reviews them in response to any questions students raise (see notes following). T makes sure to read the 16 words out loud, emphasizing pronunciation, intonation, and so on.

2. T reads out the directions on H/O #1 for part 2., with the example.

3. Ss complete the 9 squares with target words/phrases, adding definitions or notes.

4. Pairs review words together, for a set a number of minutes (likely not completing all).

5. T stops the activity and asks for interesting definitions or examples Ss heard in pairs.

Teacher Notes: Handout #1, part 2., target vocabulary and possible sentences

adopted (adj) an adopted child is legally part of a family. *My adopted brother Chris is younger.*

brother-/sister-in-law (n) brother/sister of your spouse. *Her brother-in-law is a great cook!*

engaged (adj) a person who has agreed to marry someone. *He is engaged to be married to Jane.*

extended family (n) family group with parents, children, grandparents, aunts/uncles, cousins, etc. *Her extended family is quite large and includes about 50 people all together.*

fiancé(e) (n) a man/woman who is going to marry. *Sue and fiancé Bob get married next month!*

foster child (adj) a child taken in but not legally adopted. *Their foster child Jan really fits in well.*

half-brother/-sister (n) a brother/sister with whom you share one parent. *Joe is my half-brother.*

in-laws (n) relatives by marriage, esp. the parents. *My in-laws treat me like their very own son.*

maternal/paternal (adj) relating to the mother/father. *Her maternal uncle is a famous poet.*

a middle child (n) between the oldest and youngest. *She's the middle child, between two brothers.*

an orphan (n) a child whose parents have died. *He was an orphan who was adopted at 9 months.*

to remarry (v) to marry again. *After his wife died, he chose to never remarry, and stayed single.*

sibling (n) formal, for a brother or sister. *From the same family, those siblings are so different!*

step-mother/-father (n) the wife/husband of your parent, who is not your parent. *Despite the stereotype of an evil stepmother, my dad's second wife is caring, kind, and friendly.*

to be unmarried (adj) to not be married/to be single. *Despite many suitors, she's still unmarried.*

widow/widower (n) a woman/man whose spouse died. *His wife died last year; he is a widower.*

4. Communicative Practice—Class Mingle and Speaking Practice

a. *Objectives*

— Ss review and practice known family-related vocabulary with partners

— Ss use family-related vocabulary as they learn about their classmates

— Ss receive and provide feedback on the use of family-related words

b. *Time*: 15 minutes

c. *Interaction*: T explanation, pair work, class mingle, and debrief

d. *Materials*: Student handout (H/O) #2 (Family—Find Someone Who . . .)

e. *Procedures*

1. T asks students to focus on H/O #2 and explains that there are 10 family-related scenarios. Ss are to use family words or phrases to ask and answer various questions.

2. T reads out the directions on H/O #2, with the example. Students should mingle and try to complete as many of the 10 scenarios as possible, taking notes.

3. Ss mingle and collect up to 10 names from their dialogues (likely not completing all 10).

4. T sets a timer for a particular number of minutes. T observes S pairs interacting on family.

5. T stops the activity and debriefs it by asking for examples of some interesting things Ss learned about their classmates and their family activities, expectations, and situations.

f. *Possible follow up*: Ask students to answer the following questions and to note the answers:

— *What were the most **useful** words/phrases for you in today's lesson?*

— *What were the most **difficult** words/phrases for you in today's lesson? Why?* (e.g., orphan—a new word to me, pronunciation, and spelling)

g. *Potential homework*: Students might write a journal entry on family based on class activities, and use 8 to 10 words/phrases discussed in class, highlighting (e.g., underlining) them.

Handout #1   Family Vocabulary

1. a. Use https://www.ldoceonline.com/ to fill in the blanks in the chart below.
        Check the *word family* list at the top of each entry for these words. Place an
        "X" if no such form exists.

Word Families

Noun	Adjective	Adverb	Verb
			to adopt
brother			
	divorced		
	married		
		relatively	

   b. Write good sentences with 1 word from each word family, with forms that
       are new to you!

2. Choose **9** family-related words/phrases that you would like to *review*, but
    include **5** from the list below. Write them in boxes next to the numbers 1–9,
    with any definitions or reminders to yourself. Find a partner to guess a word
    and offer a hint. For *example*: "This person is my brother's daughter, and I love
    her so much!" "She's your niece." "Correct!" If the person guesses correctly, put
    a checkmark next to that number (your partner can, too, if it is on his or her
    chart). Take turns giving hints and checking off words until one of you gets
    9 checkmarks!

adopted	brother-/sister-in-law	(to be) engaged	extended family
fiancé(e)	foster child/parent	half-brother/-sister	in-laws
maternal/paternal	a middle child	an orphan	to remarry
sibling	step-mother/-father	(to be) unmarried	widow/widower

Vocabulary Pair Work Review

1. _____ _____	2. _____ _____	3. _____ _____
4. _____ _____	5. _____ _____	6. _____ _____
7. _____ _____	8. _____ _____	9. _____ _____

Handout #2 Family—Find Someone Who . . .

Our textbook introduced family activities, expectations, and relationships. To practice what you learned and to develop fluency with relevant words and phrases you already knew, go around the class and talk to as many people as possible before you hear the bell. Ask questions to find someone who has these family experiences. Write down his or her name in the space provided and ask follow-up questions to learn more. Take notes in the space provided, and be sure to answer a question for each person you speak with too! Be ready to share what you learned!

Prompt: Is married   How long?   To whom?   How did they meet?

Sample dialogue: Ann: Hi, José, are you married?
                    José: No, but I'm divorced.
                    Ann: Sorry, how long were you married?
                    José: For 3 years, not very long.

Find someone who . . .

1. Comes from a large family   Name: _____
   How many people? Are they close?

2. Has parents who've been married 30+ years   Name: _____
   How many years? Where did they meet?

3. Wants to be a stay-at-home dad   Name: _____
   How many children? Why? For how long?

4. Is an only child   Name: _____
   Have many cousins? Wishes for a brother/sister?

5. Has grown children   Name: _____
   How old? What do they do? Where?

6. Thinks their family is ideal   Name: _____
   Why? In what way(s)? Best part?

7. Has 3 or more generations at home   Name: _____
   Who? Why? What does he or she like about it?

8. Whose mother works full time   Name: _____
   Where? How long? Type of job?

9. Has a famous family member   Name: _____
   Who? How are they famous? Close?

10. Wants to remain single   Name: _____
    Why? Other roles in their family?